FELLWALKING
WITH A CAMERA

This book is dedicated to the man who made it possible: Ken Shepherd, a photographer friend who applied his skill to my indifferent snapshots, gave them life and revealed in them a merit I had not suspected.

FELLWALKING
WITH A CAMERA

A Wainwright

WG

Westmorland Gazette, Kendal, Cumbria.

First published 1988

ISBN 0 902272 77 2

Printed by Titus Wilson & Son Ltd.,
Redmayne Yard, Stricklandgate, Kendal, Cumbria

**Published by Westmorland Gazette,
22 Stricklandgate, Kendal, Cumbria.**

INTRODUCTION

When I left Blackburn for Kendal in 1941 I was given a folding camera as a going-away present. It was a simple instrument, an improvement on the box camera I had used until then but of course it lacked the automatic devices of modern cameras. It had a moveable shutter and the exposure time could be adjusted, but for most of its life it was set at f8 and a fiftieth of a second, which was just about right for my purposes.

I took the camera with me on all my fell walks, not with the object of photographing distant landscapes and recording dramatic effects, but merely to get pictures of items of interest I met on my travels for conversion later into pen and ink drawings.

I was always disappointed with the prints I got back from the chemist where I had taken my films for processing; they were flat, dull, lacked sparkle and the sky was always a blank. They had no merit at all, obviously having been mass-produced without regard to individual treatment. Most of them had the detail I wanted, however, and I accepted the fact that I was a very mediocre photographer. I never looked at the negatives until one day, in despair upon receiving a set of prints that were pathetically poor, I compared them with the negatives and, to my surprise, found the latter to be sharp and distinct, even having clouds. So the fault lay not in developing the films, nor in me or my camera, but in the printing of the excellent negatives. I checked earlier efforts and in all cases the negatives were good but the resulting prints insipid and lifeless.

I took some of the negatives to a photographer friend and asked him to make a few specimen enlargements from them. This he did with results that amazed me. He produced excellent pictures that made me seem to be a good man with the camera and not the duffer the chemist had led me to believe. After that I entrusted all my best negatives to my friend and with new confidence extended the range of my subjects to distant landscapes and even panoramas.

It is these enlargements I have collected together to compile this book. A few are lacking in sharpness of definition and clarity, a defect I hope readers will attribute to the haze that so often shrouds the fells, but most will revive memories of happy days on the fells of this most beautiful part of the country.

A.W.

On the eastern fringe of the Lake District, between Haweswater and the A6, rises a rough tangle of moors and minor heights, an upland wilderness dissected by the valleys of Swindale and Wet Sleddale and generally referred to as Shap Fells. Although pathless and rarely visited by walkers, this high ground has several distinctive summits, all named and cairned. Of these, the rocky top of Hare Shaw in Naddle Forest is the most spectacular.

HARE SHAW, NADDLE FOREST

SADGILL, LONGSLEDDALE

The narrow motor road in Longsleddale ends after an enchanting journey of six miles from the A6 at the little community of Sadgill, where a farmhouse and a few cottages form the last outpost in the valley. With the growth of fellwalking as a pastime and the advent of the motor car, this once-quiet backwater suffers a daily invasion of visitors and their parked cars on the verges near the bridge often cause annoyance to the residents. Car parks are always a blot on the Lakeland landscape but here there really is a need for one.

Harter Fell dominates Mardale, its formidable cliffs, seamed by deep gullies, abruptly terminating the valley. To add to its distinctions of stature and bulk, Harter Fell achieved fame, kept secret at the time, as the mountain selected by the first golden eagles to return to Lakeland after an absence of 150 years: this happened in 1968 but the eyrie they built was disturbed and abandoned. Nothing daunted, they have since made their home on a crag a few miles distant. The summit, easily reached from Nan Bield Pass, has a magnificent full-length view of Haweswater.

HARTER FELL, MARDALE

On the ascent of Harter Fell from Nan Bield Pass an aerial view of Small Water is revealed, cradled in a hollow a thousand feet below. Baddeley described this lovely sheet of water as "an almost perfect specimen of a mountain tarn", and seen from above where it often appears as a glittering jewel in a rugged crown, the scene merits high praise. Beyond, a mile distant, is the head of Haweswater with an ugly tidemark that betrays its new use as a reservoir.

SMALL WATER, MARDALE

BLEA WATER CRAG, HIGH STREET

High Street, although the loftiest and most extensive mountain in the far eastern sector of the district, has few natural features along its broad top to excite the interest of visitors, but on the east side there is drama where the summit suddenly collapses in a downfall of crags to reveal, far below, a large tarn of circular outline in a deep hollow ringed by steep slopes. This is Blea Water, supposedly occupying the crater of an ancient volcano. The crags above it are broken by stony gullies but should be avoided by walkers; there have been two fatalities here.

The gathering grounds of the streams entering the head of Haweswater are the two prominent heights on the watershed beyond. Harter Fell is well known, less in popular favour is Mardale Ill Bell; between the two is Nan Bield Pass. Terraces of crags repel direct ascent although a way to the top may be found by trial and error, but the usual practice is to take a path leaving the Pass.

MARDALE ILL BELL

All the mountain tops in Lakeland are crowned by piles of stones known as cairns; some small, some large, some loosely thrown together, some built with professional care. Many of the cairns on the fells were erected by shepherds as identifiable landmarks in mist but most of those on the highest points of the summits can be attributed to walkers exuberant at their success on reaching the objective of their climb; summit cairns are always greeted with satisfaction after the effort of attaining them and many walkers perform the ritual of adding a stone. The summit of Ill Bell, small in extent, is unusually distinguished by having several mature cairns and a rash of infants.

THE SUMMIT OF ILL BELL

The usual approach to the Ill Bell ridge is from the top of Garburn Pass, reached from Kentmere village, and indeed is so steep on both sides that no other routes of ascent are practicable. A path links the three summits of Yoke, Ill Bell and Froswick, the ridge culminating at a higher level in Thornthwaite Crag, seen in the picture from the cairn on Froswick. Thornthwaite Crag can be identified from long distances, even from Kendal twelve miles away, by its handsome fourteen foot obelisk of stones, a monument to the unknown craftsman who built it. The ridge permits of no deviations, but a good alternative return to the village is available by walking east from Thornthwaite Crag and passing over Mardale Ill Bell to Nan Bield for a simple descent by a good path.

THORNTHWAITE CRAG

THE TROUTBECK VALLEY

There are many Tongues in Lakeland, all of them narrow wedges of high or rising ground between enclosing becks, the best known being the upthrust of land that divides the valley of Troutbeck. Although of modest altitude only and closely overlooked by the greater heights of Ill Bell and Caudale Moor, the summit has a glorious view down the valley, the emerald pastures and copses of woodland leading the eye to the distant waters of Windermere. The ascent of Troutbeck Tongue and the traverse of its ridge makes an interesting and rewarding half-day's expedition, the return preferably being made by a lovely path alongside Trout Beck on the western side.

THE PATTERDALE VALLEY

There are few fairer scenes than that of the Patterdale valley as seen from the rising path to Boardale Hause. Below is the green strath of cultivated pastures interspersed with mature trees, a sylvan harmony emphasised by the sombre enclosing heights. Brothers Water is glimpsed in the middle distance, and beyond, closing the horizon, Kirkstone Pass. In the space of a few miles the transition from controlled beauty to undisciplined wildness is absolute.

To travellers along the Patterdale valley, Brothers Water is a familiar sight. The road passes alongside, but full appreciation of its idyllic situation is reserved for walkers on the fellsides above and especially for those on the path between Boardale Hause and Angle Tarn who are rewarded with exquisite glimpses of the lake and the fine array of mountains around.

BROTHERS WATER

Winter travellers over Kirkstone Pass often find that Red Screes has
acquired ermine robes and assumed a new majesty and alpine splendour;
a mantle of snow covers the runs of red screes falling from the summit
ridge and from which the name of the mountain was derived. It has been
known as Red Screes ever since walkers first ventured on the fells but the
Ordnance Survey have adopted it, half-heartedly, only recently, hitherto
preferring the irrelevant name of Kilnshaw Chimney.

RED SCREES

GRISEDALE

Deeply inurned between high mountain ranges, Grisedale is a splendid springboard for walkers from Patterdale intent on climbing the peaks overlooking the valley, the most popular ascents being to St. Sunday Crag and Fairfield on the left, and Helvellyn via Striding Edge on the right. The valley also offers an interesting through route, the beautiful lower reaches giving place to the wild surroundings at its head where Grisedale Tarn and Grisedale Hause point the way to a delightful descent to the vale of Grasmere.

From the top of Fairfield there is an impressive prospect of the massive bulk of the Helvellyn range, the main summit being seen distantly above its nearer satellites of Dollywaggon Pike and Nethermost Pike. The feature commanding most attention is the great downfall of Falcon Crag immediately opposite, where the slopes of Dollywaggon Pike abruptly plunge into a gloomy recess in perpetual shadow. This scene is better viewed from a lower elevation on Fairfield which brings into sight also the path from Grisedale Tarn far below.

DOLLYWAGGON PIKE

STRIDING EDGE, HELVELLYN

There was a time when Striding Edge was regarded as a place for experienced walkers exclusively and then only in calm conditions. Today its rocky spine is crossed almost daily by pedestrians of all ages, often in parties, and indeed stories reach me of queues forming to enter upon the track that runs just below the crest and makes the passage easy. In wild weather conditions, however, it is best left alone, ice and gales being enemies. The Edge ends in a steep, loose slope leading to the broad top of Helvellyn, from where this photograph was taken.

The northern extremity of the Helvellyn range terminates abruptly at Clough Head, from where the ground falls away in a fringe of crags before descending gently to the wide valley of the River Greta. From the summit there is a superb view of Blencathra directly opposite but the fell is best known for the tremendous facade of Wanthwaite Crags, a huge rock wall overlooking St. John's in the Vale, split by the ravine of Sandbed Gill and having disused slate quarries along the base. An old track, Fisher's Wife Rake, slants upwards across the face of the crags, offering an exciting route (if it can be located) to easier ground.

CLOUGH HEAD

THE CAIRN ON SERGEANT MAN

Topping the bare and undulating moorland that feeds Easedale Tarn is the fine cairn on Sergeant Man, the only landmark from which walkers in the vicinity can take their bearings. The usual route of ascent is from Grasmere, following the well worn and often over-populated path to Easedale Tarn and continuing thence up the wide hollow between Blea Rigg and Tarn Crag. Shyly hidden off route is Codale Tarn, reached by a short detour. The Langdale Pikes come into view as height is gained but the dreary foreground detracts from the prospect in other directions.

Behold the only Lakeland summit on which I have never reached the highest point. Being always alone and over-anxious to avoid mishaps to life and limb, I have on repeated visits failed to summon up enough courage to venture up the huge pinnacle that marks the ultimate inches of Helm Crag. I am assured the climb is easy, and indeed it has been galling to watch children scrambling up to the dizzy top, but comfort myself with the consoling reflection that I am still alive and unscathed by injury. Still, I wish I had done it, just once.

THE SUMMIT OF HELM CRAG

LANGDALE PIKES, from Chapel Stile

On close acquaintance, as here seen from Chapel Stile, the Langdale Pikes assume a majestic stature and a towering presence above the flat pastures of the valley. Most prominent of the rocky heights seen from the viewpoint is Harrison Stickle, the highest of the group, closely defined by the ravines of Dungeon Ghyll and Mill Gill (Ghyll being a romantic adaptation of Gill, both denoting steep water courses), with Thorn Crag to its left and the dark cliff of Pavey Ark to its right. Few people carrying cameras pass this scene without taking a picture.

One route of approach to the heights of Langdale from the valley of the Rothay, avoiding roads and traffic, and of greater appeal, follows the high shoulder of land extending westwards from Silver How and visiting Blea Rigg on the way, enjoying superb views that are denied to the motorist and passing charming natural features that only fellwalkers are privileged to see.

LANGDALE PIKES, from Silver How

The Langdale Pikes are an arresting sight from many viewpoints in and around Great Langdale but no aspect of them surpasses that seen from the slopes of Lingmoor Fell, where their stark outline is softened by a frame of pines to make a composition of romantic beauty with all the Pikes clearly defined.

LANGDALE PIKES, from Lingmoor Fell

The frontal view of the Langdale Pikes from the minor height of Side Pike across the valley of Great Langdale, reveals in intimate detail the ruggedness of the southern aspect of the group and the distinctive summits together known as The Pikes. From the left these are Pike o' Stickle, Loft Crag, Thorn Crag, Harrison Stickle (the highest), and Pavey Ark. On the floor of the valley, disregarding threats of landslides or avalanches, is the little community of Dungeon Ghyll.

LANGDALE PIKES, from Side Pike

THE LANGDALE PIKES, from Glaramara

Those visitors who know the Langdale Pikes only by their dominating presence in the valley of Great Langdale will be surprised by their appearance when seen from other directions. In this view from Glaramara they are almost unrecognisable, seeming to be merely minor undulations on the lofty moorland extending northwards from their rugged crests.

Highest of the Langdale Pikes, Harrison Stickle overlooks the others from a middle position. Its top is attained by a roundabout route, steep crags making a direct assault too difficult to contemplate. A stone axe chipping site was found on the steep slope bordering the upper ravine of Dungeon Ghyll below the summit. Harrison Stickle, like the other Pikes, reserves its most fearsome aspect for Great Langdale, the hinterland beyond their summits being an uninteresting moorland with few landmarks. This view of it, dark in shadow, is from the sunlit cairn on Pike o' Stickle.

HARRISON STICKLE

LOFT CRAG

Looking from Pike o' Stickle to its nearest neighbour, Loft Crag, eyes are inevitably drawn to the immense buttress of naked rock that supports the slender summit. This is Gimmer Crag, the best-known of the rock climbing grounds in Great Langdale, with many severe routes on its steep front and even steeper sides, sufficiently daunting to keep mere walkers at a distance.

The unremitting steepness of the Langdale Pikes is well illustrated in this view from The Band on Bowfell, looking across Mickleden. The skyline is formed by Pike o' Stickle on the left and Loft Crag on the right, both summits appearing above a rocky fringe. Bordering Pike o' Stickle is the stony gully where the first stone axes were found.

PIKE O' STICKLE AND LOFT CRAG

Great Langdale is a valley much favoured by rock climbers with a wide choice of crags on which to practice their sport. The longest and most difficult of these climbing grounds is Gimmer Crag, reached across steep slopes below Loft Crag. Gimmer is almost severed from the fellside by the deep cleft shown in the picture: this is negotiable by non-climbing walkers but may lead into trouble and should be avoided. The opposite side of Gimmer Crag, overlooking the Pike o' Stickle scree gully, also has a sheer rock wall with many severe routes.

GIMMER CRAG

PIKE O' STICKLE

Pike o' Stickle is the most shapely of the Langdale Pikes, an unremitting steep slope, terraced by crags, leaping from the valley of Mickleden to a small neat dome, this being the aspect most often seen. The summit is usually reached by a detour from the well-trodden path to Harrison Stickle; a direct ascent, more laborious, may be made up the stony gully alongside. It was at the top of this gully that traces of a neolithic stone axe factory were first discovered, other nearby sites being brought to light later, and the pioneers were rewarded by finding several specimens of this primitive implement. Since then, walkers have combined the ascent with a search for stone axes, often successfully.

Thorn Crag is rounded by the path to Harrison Stickle, a circuitous route to avoid rough ground, and its summit is rarely visited and indeed has little of interest, although once, at dusk, I saw a young fox there having lots of fun rolling on its back and chasing its tail. Along the eastern side of the fell, and often passed unnoticed, is the deep canyon formed by the headwaters of Dungeon Ghyll, a grim place lined by crags and one of the few secrets of the district not yet frequented by countless thousands who every year pass nearby with their eyes fixed on their main objective, Harrison Stickle.

THORN CRAG

PAVEY ARK, from Harrison Stickle

Viewed from Harrison Stickle, Pavey Ark is seen in profile, its cliffs plunging down to Stickle Tarn in a series of buttresses broken by steep gullies. Despite its forbidding appearance, however, Pavey Ark has a benign summit, easily reached by a simple traverse. In the background of the view, across the intermediate heights of Sergeant Man and Blea Rigg, is the long skyline of the Helvellyn range.

So named but not exactly a simple passage for genteel pedestrians, Easy Gully splits the crags at the northern end of Pavey Ark into a great rift negotiable with little difficulty except at one point where a huge chockstone bars progress. This gully offers a short cut to the top of the fell from Stickle Tarn. From the upper part the view downwards extends over Stickle Tarn to the distant heights of the Coniston Fells.

EASY GULLY, PAVEY ARK

Before Gimmer Crag attained its present great popularity with Langdale's rock climbers, Pavey Ark was the main attraction of devotees of the sport, its fearful precipices enhanced by the dark waters of Stickle Tarn below. Pavey Ark still yields many difficult climbs and for active walkers has a safe but rather desperate scramble in Jack's Rake, a terrace sloping across the sheer face of the crags to easier ground above. Once relatively unknown, today one hears of queues forming to attempt Jack's Rake and prove themselves men. Stickle Tarn was once used as a reservoir for a gunpowder works at Elterwater.

PAVEY ARK

Great Langdale divides at its head into two branches, Oxendale and Mickleden, the latter valley traversed by a popular path to Rossett Gill en route for Wasdale and Scafell Pike. The climb up the gill is stony and arduous with good retrospective views of the valley and Pike o' Stickle. On a nearby knoll a simple cross of stones laid on the ground marks the grave of a packwoman who perished here two centuries ago.

MICKLEDEN

FISHER CRAG, THIRLMERE

Until Manchester Corporation extended their plantations along the sides of Thirlmere, the fine viewpoint illustrated could be attained easily from the open moor of Armboth Fell; today it must be regarded as out of bounds. This is a pity, depriving walkers of a splendid aerial view of the lake and Blencathra beyond framed between Raven Crag and Clough Head.

Best known of the dozen Eagle Crags in Lakeland, this one forming a massive cornerstone at the confluence of the Greenup and Langstrath valleys is most interesting to climb, progress being made by trial and error through the terraced crags barring a direct ascent. The effort is worth while, the summit rocks making a delightful perch. The approach to it along the lovely Stonethwaite valley is a joy to tread.

EAGLE CRAG

THE SUMMIT OF EAGLE CRAG

After finding a way through the maze of crags that give Eagle Crag so formidable an appearance when viewed from the Stonethwaite valley, those who succeed in reaching the highest point of the fell are surprised to find that the actual summit is a tilted slab with a small cairn delicately poised on its edge. Apart from its merits as a couch for a siesta or a table for a picnic, the view from this airy perch of the Stonethwaite valley and Borrowdale makes all the effort of getting here well worth while.

Langstrath is a popular link for foot-travellers between Great Langdale and Borrowdale by way of Stake Pass and a striking feature of this interesting journey is the precipice of Sergeant's Crag, a tower of dark cliffs above runs of scree. The top is obviously unattainable by a direct climb by any other than expert cragsmen, but in fact is easily gained from the hinterland of Langdale Pikes. A simple ridge connects the summit with nearby Eagle Crag.

SERGEANT'S CRAG

All the valleys in Lakeland are fair to look upon and I love every one but my very special favourite is the mile-long offshoot of Borrowdale in which nestles the old settlement of Stonethwaite, a picturesque group of stone buildings in a setting of great charm. Seen from the confining heights the valley is an oasis of fertility sheltered by shaggy fells, Dale Head being the most prominent from this viewpoint high on the climb to Dock Tarn.

THE STONETHWAITE VALLEY

Borrowdale is endowed with many scenes of exquisite natural beauty and the path coming over from Watendlath reveals one of the fairest. The middle reaches of the valley are displayed to perfection, emerald pastures contrasting with dark woodlands as the valley curves to its beginnings watched over by Lingmell and Great Gable.

BORROWDALE, from the Watendlath path

King's How was purchased and so named as a memorial to King Edward VII, and who could wish for a better tribute? This delightful height, part of Grange Fell, rises steeply above the Jaws of Borrowdale and commands a superb full-length view of that loveliest of Lakeland's valleys, from the peaks ranged around its source to Derwentwater backed by the Skiddaw group. The ascent from Troutdale too abounds in delightful situations, a ladder of rocks and heather among trees and bushes in a colourful medley.

THE SUMMIT OF KING'S HOW

The narrow road to Watendlath rises beyond Ashness Bridge to enter a natural woodland, a home of the red squirrel, and from stances alongside there are bewitching glimpses of Derwentwater below and the verdant Vale of Keswick watered by the River Derwent on its way to enter Bassenthwaite Lake. Some care is necessary at these well patronised viewpoints, the ground breaking away into dangerous cliffs.

THE VALE OF KESWICK

One of the most photographed scenes in Lakeland is the perfect composition provided by the picturesque Ashness Bridge on the romantic road to Watendlath. Had the scene been specially designed for the camera it could not have been better; it is a gem. The Skiddaw group form an impressive background to a beautiful view.

ASHNESS BRIDGE

DERWENTWATER IN WINTER

Walking on Derwentwater is an experience unknown to summer visitors but the relatively few who come in a winter gripped by hard frost and snow find the lake transformed into a fairyland of ethereal beauty amid frozen landscapes of virgin purity. To my mind winter has always been the best time to enjoy Lakeland and has become increasingly so as the passing years have seen an escalating flood of holiday tourists and day trippers. Lakeland was not made for crowds.

Walla Crag is not high by mountain standards and its summit can be reached by a gentle stroll, but as a viewpoint for Derwentwater it excels. The lake is directly below and beyond the far shore the fells of the northwest form a majestic background, Causey Pike and Grisedale Pike being especially prominent.

DERWENTWATER, from Walla Crag

DERWENTWATER, from Castle Head

Most visitors to Keswick are content to view Derwentwater from Friar's Crag at shore level, and a splendid scene it is. But a grander one is revealed from the top of the nearby hill, Castle Head, reached with little effort from the Borrowdale road on a well-trodden and winding path through a mature woodland to its bare and rocky top.

From the top of Coniston Old Man an exhilarating high level traverse can be made along the obvious ridge to the north, as seen in the photograph, passing over the gentle dome of Brim Fell and, after a descent to the depression of Levers Hause, rising to the culmination of the ridge at Swirl How, a few feet higher than the Old Man. Throughout this walk the western slopes are bland and uninteresting but the eastern side falls away in rough declivities broken by crags. It is usual to complete the round by continuing to Wetherlam but an intermediate return to Coniston is available by way of Levers Water.

THE MAIN RIDGE OF THE CONISTON FELLS

The ascent of the Old Man is performed almost as a ritual by visitors to Coniston village, its dominating presence demanding the attention of all active walkers. The much trodden path to the top, steep in the final stages, often carries a procession of pedestrians of all ages and it is quite usual to find a crowd congregated on the stone platform from which there is a wide prospect over Morecambe Bay, and landward a great array of mountains with the Scafells prominent in the distance.

THE SUMMIT OF CONISTON OLD MAN

With the sights and sounds of industrial exploitation left behind, the top of Coniston Old Man still retains an atmosphere of undisturbed peace when its crowds of summer visitors have departed, or in winter when a mantle of snow deters all but a few hardy walkers from making the ascent. Then the Old Man is at his best, supremely poised above a white world.

THE TOP OF CONISTON OLD MAN

DOW CRAG IN WINTER

Dow Crag, separated from Coniston Old Man by a deep hollow containing Goats Water, has long had a reputation as a major climbing ground for experienced cragsmen and is a great favourite amongst those who practice the sport of rock climbing, a variety of routes leading up to the pile of rocks forming the summit and poised above the fearful abyss. Here it is seen from the Old Man, the link between the two mountains being provided by Goats Hause on the right.

Due to severe foreshortening it is difficult to appreciate the true dimensions of Dow Crag from the path by Goats Water along the base of the mountain, but a grandstand view is obtained from the slopes of Coniston Old Man directly opposite and at a similar elevation. From here the buttresses and gullies that make this one of the finest climbing grounds for rock climbers are in evidence and the peaked summit, attainable by lesser mortals but not visible from below, is clearly seen.

DOW CRAG, CONISTON

BRIM FELL

Brim Fell has no terrors for walkers content to stroll across its easy top but, hidden from the sight of those who do this without straying from the path, is an accompanying line of crags that spell trouble for anyone attempting a direct descent. This view, taken from the rising ground beyond Levers Hause, includes Dow Crag's summit on the extreme right.

The walk over the top of Brim Fell is an easy promenade with little of immediate interest but enriched by splendid views in all directions; there is little awareness of the crags that fall away sharply from the eastern edge. Brim Fell is the first summit on the main ridge of the Coniston Fells northwards from the Old Man to which it is linked by a slight depression. Beyond the cairn there is a long descent to the gap of Levers Hause followed by a steady climb, skirting the rim of Little How Crags and Great How Crags, to the level top of Swirl How. In the picture Swirl How is the highest point on the skyline.

THE SUMMIT OF BRIM FELL

GREAT CARRS

Walkers arriving at the top of Swirl How from the south are faced by the dark precipice of Great Carrs, its impossible cliffs debouching rivers of scree into the Greenburn valley far below. In one of the many gullies may still be seen the wrecked fusilage of an aeroplane that failed to clear the top of the fell. Away from the line of crags, however, Great Carrs offers an easy and pleasant ridge walk with access to or from Wrynose Pass.

WETHERLAM, from Great Carrs

A popular expedition from Coniston village follows the height of land on a circular tour around the horseshoe of fells that fill the sky to the west. The usual route lies along the north ridge from the Old Man, turning east from Swirl How to reach the top of Wetherlam, from which a parallel ridge gives an easy descent back to the village. Wetherlam is a bulky fell, cruelly exploited in past years for its mineral wealth, as a honeycomb of shafts and levels on its lower slopes, all disused and abandoned, still mutely testify.

The northern aspect of the Coniston Fells is well seen from the slopes of Lingmoor Fell across the hollow carrying the road to Wrynose Pass. The most prominent height in view is Wetherlam with the more distant ridge of Great Carrs to the right. Nearer, the dark cliffs of Black Crag seen rising out of the picture, culminate ultimately in the summit of Pike o' Blisco.

THE NORTHERN CONISTON FELLS

Less frequented than its popular neighbour, Great Langdale, and having a shyness the other lacks, Little Langdale nonetheless has a charm all its own. The narrow road reveals scenes of natural beauty around every corner and a shining jewel in its midst where a tarn mirrors the gaunt outline of the fells behind; of these,Wetherlam is the most prominent in view and the descending ridge from Swirl How to Wrynose Pass is also well seen.

LITTLE LANGDALE

Slaters Bridge in Little Langdale is the most primitive and yet picturesque arch in the district. Constructed wholly of slate, it was built originally to provide for the quarry men who worked in the adjoining slate quarries a short route to their homes in the valley. In the background of this picture is Lingmoor Fell.

SLATERS BRIDGE, LITTLE LANGDALE

PIKE O' BLISCO

Pike o' Blisco has little claim to distinction of outline but seen from The Band on Bowfell, as here, assumes the shape of a graceful pyramid; it also once had a graceful summit cairn, a work of art. It was here that I first had evidence that the vandals of the towns had arrived on the mountain tops. The cairn, having withstood the storms of centuries, I found wantonly destroyed. An appeal for volunteers to restore it found a ready response although the efforts of amateurs lacked the professional skill of the forgotten dalesman who built the original.

The serrated summit ridge of Crinkle Crags is a conspicuous feature of the skyline around the head of Great Langdale. From a distance the many ups and downs on the top of the fell seem minor and innocuous, but this appearance is deceptive and walkers engaged on the full traverse, an exhilarating expedition, find the undulations profound and conditions underfoot extremely rough and stony. The viewpoint of the picture is Oxendale, a branch of Great Langdale: a direct ascent may be made from this point but it is more usual to take a circuitous route by way of Red Tarn below Pike o' Blisco.

CRINKLE CRAGS

CRINKLE CRAGS AND BOWFELL

The usual route of ascent of Crinkle Crags is by a climb from Oxendale or, much more easily, from the motor road at Wrynose Pass, skirting the shores of Red Tarn on the way. From here a clear path goes up the slope on the left, rounds the top of the first large crag, Great Knott, and then rises gradually to the first of the five Crinkles, the other four following in succession on a thrilling crossing with superlative views. Bowfell rises in isolation at the end of the Crinkles ridge.

Crinkle Crags, seen at close quarters, is an uncompromising desert of rock and scree with no invitation to walkers to explore its wild inner recesses and near-vertical cliffs. Arduous ascents may be made up the stony gullies but with no feeling of the exhilaration experienced by following the path over the various tops.

CRINKLE CRAGS, from Pike o' Blisco

THE PATH ON CRINKLE CRAGS

A stony but fascinating path crosses all the Crinkles, one after another, on a switchback tour of infinite delight to walkers who are shod sensibly; this is no place for sandals. All the tops have excellent views, Great Langdale appearing as from an aeroplane. The highest Crinkle, Long Top, is in the background of this picture, taken on the approach from Three Tarns.

The highest summit of the Crinkles is named Long Top and on attaining it Bowfell comes into view to the north, its appearance daunting, the facing slope having a long line of cliffs broken by a series of gullies known as the Links, each choked by boulders and scree. The foreground is characteristic of the Crinkles, rough walking on ground littered by stones through which generations of walkers have trodden a distinct path; without its help the crossing of the Crinkles would be a strenuous exercise.

BOWFELL, from Crinkle Crags

This is an aspect of Bowfell familiar to all fellwalkers. Looking from the lower slopes of Shelter Crags across the depression of Three Tarns, attention is centred on the long line of cliffs below the summit, split by a dozen parallel gullies known as the Links, all of them choked by insecure boulders and unsafe. The usual tourist path to the top from Great Langdale, blazed white by heavy foot-traffic, is seen winding up to the skyline on the right.

BOWFELL

BOWFELL BUTTRESS

The crowds who aspire to the summit of Bowfell invariably follow the worn path up the final pyramid above Three Tarns but a discerning minority prefer an exciting detour along the Climbers' Traverse, a thin track leading across the side of the mountain and passing below Flat Crags to Cambridge Crag, where a reward awaits in the form of a spring of water that gushes like a fountain from the rocks at its base. At this point Bowfell Buttress comes into clear view directly ahead, a towering pillar of rock that provides sport for expert climbers but is obviously no place for ordinary mortals. From the traverse the summit can be reached by a scramble up a boulder-strewn stairway between Flat Crags and Cambridge Crag.

Pike o' Blisco has a grandstand view of its near neighbours Bowfell and Crinkle Crags, the steep declivities falling into Oxendale being impressively seen. Cutting deep into the side of The Band on Bowfell is the huge cleft of Hell Gill with a notable waterfall hidden from the sight of all but intrepid explorers. This chasm is matched by Crinkle Gill coming down from Crinkle Crags in a series of cascades.

BOWFELL, from Pike o' Blisco

THE SCAFELL RANGE, from Grey Friar

Grey Friar is the least visited of the Coniston Fells, standing in isolation from the others and having nothing of intrinsic interest, its one great merit being the magnificent view of the Scafell range from the summit cairn. Forming a massive wall above the fastnesses of the head of Eskdale are Scafell, Scafell Pike, Broad Crag, Ill Crag and Great End - the finest high level traverse in the district.

THE SCAFELL RANGE, from Crinkle Crags

Looking across the great gulf of upper Eskdale, the view of the Scafell range from Crinkle Crags reveals all the main summits in perspective; Scafell on the left and, over the gap of Mickledore, Scafell Pike followed by Broad Crag, Ill Crag and Great End in a continuous high-level skyline around 3,000 feet in altitude.

The rough plateau of Red How affords a detailed view of the Scafell range. Scafell is the major height on the left and then across the gap of Mickledore is Scafell Pike, with Dow Crag prominent on the fellside below the summit and Ill Crag closing the skyline to the right. There is a glimpse of Broad Crag between the last two. The range is seen rising above the unseen valley of the Esk.

THE SCAFELL RANGE, from Red How

Every experienced fellwalker in Lakeland greets Stockley Bridge as an old friend, a starting and finishing point for the grandest mountain expedition of all with Scafell Pike as the objective: two alternative routes can be combined in a circular walk from here. The bridge is easily reached by a wide path from Seathwaite in Borrowdale, perhaps too easily because it is accessible without effort and therefore attracts visitors of all ages and types who picnic there with no thought of going further.

STOCKLEY BRIDGE

The centuries-old path to Sty Head and Wasdale climbs the fellside above Stockley Bridge, the original, well-grazed zig-zag path having been eroded by impatient walkers who prefer short cuts. Near the top of the slope, however, it reasserts itself and goes forward as a single track revealing a retrospective view of the upper part of Borrrowdale, the green strath in sharp contrast to the rough slopes of the bordering fells.

THE HEAD OF BORROWDALE

LINGMELL

Often bypassed by walkers en route to Scafell Pike from Wasdale, Lingmell remains subservient to its great neighbour, yet the short detour to its top more than repays the small extra effort by revealing a sensational view of Great Gable across the deep gulf of Lingmell Beck. Lingmell is also notable for the huge chasm of Piers Gill splitting its northern fellside, well seen in this picture from Sty Head.

I must write of the Lingmell cairn in the past tense. this imposing pillar of stones having been wantonly destroyed by mindless vandals who find a sadistic pleasure in wrecking the work of others. Fellwalkers with a genuine love of the hills come to regard summit cairns as sacrosanct. objectives representing achievement after effort. hallowed places inviting rest after toil. shrines that deserve respect. Later correspondents have told me of their endeavours to restore the cairn to its former handsome proportions.

THE LINGMELL CAIRN

GREAT END

The highest range of fells in the country, from Scafell Pike northwards, terminates abruptly at the well-named Great End, where a long line of cliffs plunges a thousand feet to easier ground. Crossed by the Langdale-Wasdale path near Sprinkling Tarn it forms an imposing bastion that defies direct assault but can be circumvented without serious climbing. The top commands a full-length view of Borrowdale to distant Skiddaw, a beautiful prospect and a fine reward for the effort of getting there. The viewpoint of the picture is a small, unnamed tarn on Seathwaite Fell.

Of the many alternative routes of ascent to Scafell Pike, none is more attractive than the path from Eskdale, especially in the vicinity of Throstle Garth, where the River Esk, a delightful companion on the journey, descends in waterfalls from a wild mountain surround to the loveliness of the valley. After crossing the picturesque Lingcove Bridge at a sharp turn in the course of the river, a splendid view unfolds ahead revealing Scafell Pike as a shapely pyramid with Ill Crag as a rugged neighbour.

THROSTLE GARTH, ESKDALE

SCAFELL PIKE AND ILL CRAG

An unfrequented route to Scafell Pike from Eskdale traverses the plateau north of Taw House, initially requiring a steep climb alongside Cowcove Beck, and leads easily to Great Moss and the climb to the top by way of Cam Spout and Mickledore.

From Great Moss the climb to Scafell Pike rises very steeply alongside the waterfall of Cam Spout, Scafell Pike being seen towering above and a mile further out. Although a beeline can be made to the summit over steep and pathless ground, the way usually taken by walkers is to follow the descending stream upwards to its end below the scree falling from Mickledore, which is gained after a tedious scramble. A clear path then leads to the summit.

CAM SPOUT, UPPER ESKDALE

Walkers arriving at Great Moss and bound for Scafell Pike can achieve their objective by a much more adventurous alternative to the usual path by following the Esk upstream to the narrow side valley beyond the impressive cliffs of Dow Crag, a favourite resort of rock climbers. Scrambling up this side valley, Little Narrowcove, to emerge in a strange amphitheatre in a surround of crags, the obvious escape is forward to the col between the Pike and Broad Crag, there turning left to the summit. This approach is unfrequented and reveals a savage aspect of the Pike unseen and unsuspected by travellers on the usual routes of ascent.

LITTLE NARROWCOVE, SCAFELL PIKE

The Eskdale route to Scafell reaches the base of the mountain at a large tract of flat ground, in places boggy, through which the infant Esk threads a sluggish passage. This is Great Moss, once owned by Furness Abbey as a deer pasture. From it, the path to the Pike rises in an unremitting slope of almost two thousand feet.

GREAT MOSS, UPPER ESKDALE

THE PATH TO SCAFELL PIKE

This scene, where the top of Scafell Pike comes fully into view, is greeted joyfully by walkers who see an early end to their labours but with dismay by others who have already had enough of rough walking and see ahead still another half mile of difficult travail over scree and boulders. This is the most popular route of ascent, paths from Great Langdale and Borrowdale combining on this final section. The path is seen rising across the flank of Broad Crag on the right, beyond which it disappears into a depression before climbing up to the highest ground in England.

The most impressive feature in the extensive view from Scafell Pike is the massive, shadowed face of Scafell nearby, across the small ridge of Mickledore linking the two mountains. To the right of this ridge towers the greatest and grandest crag in Lakeland, Scafell Crag, to the left is the formidable East Buttress, and in a strip of sunlight between is the notorious Broad Stand, apparently offering a direct route of ascent but failing to do so on closer acquaintance. The average walker can reach the top of Scafell in safety only by wide detours around the crags.

SCAFELL

The edge of Lingmell overlooking Brown Tongue commands a view of the most dramatic scenery in the Scafell range. On the left, Pikes Crag abruptly terminates the high mass of Scafell Pike, and on the right towers the near-vertical rock wall of Scafell Crag, the summit of Scafell being seen beyond the upper cliffs. Linking the two mountains is the slender ridge of Mickledore in a depression of the skyline above the grassy and bouldery amphitheatre of Hollow Stones.

SCAFELL, from Lingmell

Piers Gill forms a dog-leg, the upper portion, seen here looking down, being negotiable along the stony bed, but around the corner a precipitous waterfall effectively stops further descent. It was in the gloomy depths of the gill at this point that a lost and injured walker survived for eighteen days on a trickle of water before being found. The view is from the Corridor Route, which crosses the fellside at the head of the gill.

PIERS GILL

HOLLOW STONES

On the popular ascent of Scafell Pike from Wasdale a grassy shelf is reached with Pikes Crag rearing up grandly ahead. At this point there is a choice of two routes to the summit, the more usual passing below the cliffs to the left to rise above them on a stony path, the other continuing forward into the amphitheatre of Hollow Stones and climbing steeply from there to the slender ridge of Mickledore, where a turn to the left leads upwards to the huge summit cairn. The Mickledore route passes through scenes of awesome grandeur below the immense precipice of Scafell Crag.

Most visitors to Scafell from Wasdale Head gain height by ascending the popular path up Brown Tongue at the top of which they are faced by rock scenery on a grand scale - Pikes Crag on the left and Black Crag heralding Scafell Crag on the right. The boulder-strewn amphitheatre between is Hollow Stones, providing the only easy walking hereabouts and shelter for bivouacs in the lee of tumbled boulders.

PIKES CRAG

Descent from Scafell Pike to Wasdale Head can be made with advantage by following down the curving ridge of Lingmell, a route excelling in fine views. The Scafell crags are magnificently displayed, there is a classic picture of Great Gable from the top of the gullies, and lower down a full-length prospect of Mosedale. As the descent continues, the valley gradually opens up in front revealing the whole expanse of Wastwater and beyond, on a clear day across the sea, the Isle of Man. However, the pastoral coastal area is marred by the alien nuclear power station at Sellafield.

WASDALE

Seen from Green How on Scafell, as in this picture, Illgill Head appears as a grassy dome promising an easy trudge to its summit, a climb without difficulties or hazards. The western side of this fell, however, is very different, a sudden downfall of cliffs and scree plunging steeply into the depths of Wastwater at its base. The two-mile walk along its crest has spectacular and sensational downward views into the lake and culminates to the rocky peak of Whin Rigg, split by tremendous chasms that provide rock climbs for experts only.

ILLGILL HEAD

WASTWATER SCREES

Of all the natural scenes in Lakeland provoking wonderment, awe and even fear amongst visitors, none is more spectacular than the desert of stones tumbling from the rim of crags along the edge of Illgill Head, the whole forming a tremendous facade to the mountain above the dark waters of the deepest lake of all. Many visitors of a timid disposition recoil with horror at the grim aspect facing them; when lit by late afternoon sunlight, however, it is colourful and beautiful. Near the foot of the lake the screes give way to the even grimmer cliffs of Whin Rigg.

Whin Rigg ends the high ridge bordering Wastwater in the south, the land beyond gradually descending to the pleasant woodlands and pastures of the coast. The fell overlooks the foot of the lake, from which steeply rise fans of scree topped by huge cliffs that palpably preclude ascent, only the deep gullies having been climbed by expert rock gymnasts. The summit, however, which is invariably reached by a traverse of the ridge from Illgill Head, is a delightful place, blessed with far views over the coastal plain to the sea.

WHIN RIGG

WASTWATER, from Greathall Gill

The descent southwards from the summit of Whin Rigg follows an easy slope skirting the edge of the fearful declivities that plunge down into Wasdale but on reaching the top of the great gully of Greathall Gill, also known as Hawl Gill, a way may be made down its near side to the valley clear of crags. A wonderful view of Wastwater unfolds on this descent, the whole of the lake being seen cradled in the laps of an unbroken surround of fells with Yewbarrow the most prominent and Great Gable closing the head of the valley.

The principal heights of the Scafell group are in full view and seen in perspective from Middle Dodd, the scene being enhanced by Wastwater far below. Lingmell appears on the left rising to Scafell Pike and across the depression of Hollow Stones soar the crags of Scafell. The popular route of ascent to either leads up the valley of Lingmell Gill seen immediately above the head of the lake.

THE SCAFELL GROUP, from Middle Dodd

Contrasting with the human activity around and beyond the head of Wastwater, the foot of the lake is usually undisturbed by visitors. The prospect from this quiet outflow is superb. Between the wooded promontory of Low Wood and the beetling crags of Whin Rigg is a distant horizon formed by the three peaks of Yewbarrow, Kirk Fell and the highest and grandest of the trinity - the shapely pyramid of Great Gable.

THE FOOT OF WASTWATER

Many visitors seeing Wastwater for the first time, especially if the lake is shrouded under a ceiling of storm clouds, recoil in horror at the awful gloominess of the scene, repelled by the sinister aspect of the dark waters and the petrified avalanches of stones on its far shore; some, to my knowledge, have fled vowing never to return. Yet on a sunny day in spring, when the hawthorns and the gorse are in bloom along the roadside, it is so easy to fall in love with the lake and its majestic surroundings.

THE HEAD OF WASTWATER

NETHER BECK, WASDALE

One of the great delights of fellwalking is derived from following upwards to their source the streams that come rapidly down to valley level from the heights above, often in a series of waterfalls, cascades and pools. They are jolly companions on ascents to the summits and although not usually accompanied by paths, give interesting climbing alongside. Pictured here is Nether Beck on its way down from the Pillar range to enter Wastwater.

THE ESKDALE NEEDLE

Occasionally when wandering about the fells, especially in areas off the beaten track, the walker comes unexpectedly upon strange rock formations where weathering has left some bizarre shapes. Such a place is to be found by searching the Eskdale slope of Hard Knott where, standing in isolation, is the pinnacle known as the Eskdale Needle.

It is rather a rough pull to the top of Harter Fell after the pleasant approaches from Eskdale or the Duddon valley are left behind. But joy awaits in the massive rocks adorning the summit which invite simple scrambling and, in particular, the glorious prospect of upper Eskdale and the magnificent Scafell range closing the horizon.

THE APPROACH TO HARTER FELL

HARTER FELL

Harter Fell is not numbered amongst the giants but has all the attributes of a fine mountain. It is the most prominent height in mid-Eskdale, a sentinel to the great mountains at the head of the valley. Lush slopes of bracken and heather lead up to a rocky summit with superb views. This photograph, taken from the slopes above Taw House, shows the western aspect of Harter Fell across Eskdale at Brotherilkeld.

THE SUMMIT OF HARTER FELL

Few who have climbed to the top of Harter Fell in Eskdale will have regretted the climb. The summit is fascinating, the highest point being a fang of rock on which the Ordnance Survey could find no accommodation for their triangulation column, which is sited nearby. Visitors can indulge in some mild scrambling on the topmost rocks and enjoy superlative views of the valleys of the Duddon and the Esk and particularly of upper Eskdale. It is a place to linger.

From the rocky top of Harter Fell there is an uninterrupted and comprehensive view of the higher reaches of Eskdale, a prospect of a landscape of unexcelled grandeur ringed by high mountains, the Scafells and Bowfell rising supreme above and beyond a wilderness of foothills and watercourses. This is the viewpoint above all others for studying the intricacies of upper Eskdale. Nearer, and seen as a high-flying bird would view it, is the Roman fort of Hardknott.

UPPER ESKDALE

BORROWDALE, from Thornythwaite Fell

The usual line of descent from Glaramara into Borrowdale is by way of the grassy ridge of Thornythwaite Fell and every step is made a pleasure by the entrancing picture ahead along the valley to Derwentwater, the view being closed by the Skiddaw group of fells in the far distance.

The views from Glaramara are superb in all directions and none more so than the western prospect, where Base Brown, Gillercombe Buttress and Honister Crag darkly intrude on a tangled landscape and precede the ultimate fells of High Crag in the High Stile range and Grasmoor. There is a wealth of detail in this far-reaching view needing the collaboration of a map.

THE WESTERN FELLS, from Glaramara

Seen across the gulf of Sty Head Pass the two major heights of Great
Gable and Pillar overtop all else and rise proudly into the sky. Glaramara
is privileged by its central position in the district, the views in all
directions being outstanding. The traverse of the summit ridge, enhanced by some small but attractive pools, jewels in a rocky crown, is a
delight every step of the way.

GREAT GABLE AND PILLAR, from Glaramara

Great Gable's name is itself a challenge to all fellwalkers and routes of ascent are well blazed by the boots of thousands of pilgrims annually. The most popular path can be discerned in the photograph: this is the Breast Route, leading directly to the summit from Sty Head, a straight-forward climb with no difficulties other than steepness. Since this picture was taken some thirty years ago, the foot traffic on this path has increased to such an extent that it is now of road width.

GREAT GABLE, from Great End

TOP OF THE NAPES, GREAT GABLE

This unfamiliar aspect of the rocky pinnacles of the Napes on Great Gable shows their appearance when viewed from Westmorland Crags. The thin track along the short ridge leads to a breach in the crags known as Little Hell Gate, the only safe passage for walkers, although by descending the screes to the left of the ridge, a way can be found through Great Hell Gate to the popular girdle route around the mountain.

Lingmell, among its other attributes, has a classic view of Great Gable, seen from tip to toe as a majestic pyramid of unremitting steepness appearing near-vertical and unassailable. Slanting across it is the narrow scar formed by the path from Sty Head to Wasdale; higher, less defined, is the track of Gable Girdle, passing below the ridges of the Great Napes and Kern Knotts. Seen from the rim of Lingmell's cliffs, Great Gable fully merits its name.

GREAT GABLE, from Lingmell

THE SUMMIT OF GREAT GABLE

The rocky top of Great Gable is treated with respect by the older generation of fellwalkers to whom it is hallowed ground. A tablet affixed to a rock proclaims the summit as the war memorial of the Fell and Rock Climbing Club and every year since 1924 a congregation has assembled here for a Remembrance Service in November, often numbering several hundreds and without regard to weather conditions.

Few walkers reach the summit of Great Gable without going further to the edge of Westmorland Crags, where a magnificent prospect of Wasdale and Wastwater is presented, a picture no one carrying a camera is able to resist despite the inclusion in it of the Sellafield Nuclear Power Station on the coast.

WASTWATER, from Great Gable

From the edge of Great Gable's stony summit the high skyline of the Scafell range is seen in detail as an uncompromising barrier of rough ground steepening into distinct summits and riven by descending ravines and watercourses. This is the best viewpoint for seeing the full length of the Corridor Route, a short cut to Scafell Pike from Sty Head, originated by rock climbers but now adopted by walkers; it follows the grassy shelf at mid-height in the photograph.

THE SCAFELL RANGE, from Great Gable

PILLAR

Pillar has a compelling name that draws walkers like a magnet, and if its famous Rock is included in the day's itinerary, is a journey full of excitement and interest. Pillar is one of the giants of the district, soaring proudly between Mosedale and the long valley of Ennerdale. I knew Pillar before the Ennerdale Forests came to shroud its beauty and dress it in dark green skirts. It has been cruelly humiliated. The Ennerdale Forest was a sad mistake.

On the descent to Beck Head from the summit of Great Gable, a view opens up ahead of the long afforested valley of Ennerdale but attention will be focused on the proud presence of Pillar, its long and serrated eastern ridge defined by shadow, and sharp eyes will note Pillar Rock in silhouette on the Ennerdale flank. Nearer, and below eye level, is Kirk Fell.

PILLAR AND KIRK FELL

The royal road to Pillar Rock is a path known as the High Level Traverse, pioneered by the early rock climbers a century ago and now commonly adopted by adventurers young and old, an initial difficulty having been bypassed. It is on this approach that the Rock is seen at its most impressive, rising from the fellside like a shattered cathedral, a challenge to expert climbers.

PILLAR ROCK

The top of Pillar is bare, flat and not at all pillar-like, all the excitement of this fine mountain being centred on its steep northern flank overlooking Ennerdale, where Pillar Rock towers supreme from a craggy fellside. On a clear day the distant panorama of the Scafell range also arrests the attention, the full extent of the group from Great End to Scafell being seen to perfection.

THE SUMMIT OF PILLAR

Water authorities have cast covetous eyes on Ennerdale's lake for many years but their projects for increasing the water level have twice been defeated by the spirited opposition of those who care more for Ennerdale Water than do the authorities. Today there are still paths around its shores that would otherwise have been lost. Lovely and unspoilt, it makes a fitting foreground for the lofty Pillar range overlooking it in the south.

THE PILLAR RANGE

Any approach to Pillar up the Ennerdale flank, where there are no paths to ease the climb, is rough underfoot and indeed more of a scramble than a walk but it is possible by trial and error to force a passage up the craggy slope by way of the scree gullies falling from it. The highlight of the ascent is the intimate view of the Rock from an unfamiliar angle.

PILLAR, from Ennerdale

THE RIVER LIZA, ENNERDALE

The River Liza has its beginnings on Great Gable and on its journey to join Ennerdale Water formerly flowed through an open and pleasant valley. But fifty years ago came the Forestry Commission and today the river is encompassed by dense conifer plantations that screen its delightful meanderings from view, and only in a few places is there access to its attractive rocky banks.

YEWBARROW

The benign lower slopes of Yewbarrow above Over Beck are a tempting preliminary to the ascent of this conveniently-situated fell on the shore of Wastwater, but difficulties soon appear in the cliffs of Bell Rib, which deny access to the ridge beyond. This obstacle can be avoided by contouring to the left until a scree gully offers a way upwards to very rough ground beyond the cliffs and an easy walk to the summit. Bell Rib is a notorious trap when descending from Yewbarrow.

Yewbarrow is a steep-sided mountain but not difficult to negotiate along
its crest except at both ends. At the north end of the ridge Stirrup Crag
involves a very rough scramble without hazards, but at the south end Bell
Rib is a much more serious proposition; cliffs constitute a real danger and
must be bypassed using scree gullies that connect with easier ground.

BELL RIB, YEWBARROW

RED PIKE, MOSEDALE

Walkers arriving at the summit of Red Pike along the grassy slopes rising gradually from Wastwater will be surprised and even shocked by the dramatic fall of the mountain into Mosedale in a petrified avalanche of crags. Under snow, the scene is alpine and palpably rules out a direct ascent from the valley for ill-equipped climbers.

The steep flank of Red Pike overlooking Mosedale is a shadowed tumble of crags, a no-man's-land where few walkers wander, but the top of the fell is an easy promenade along the edge of the tremendous downfall into the depths of the valley. The summit cairn, perched high above a fearful drop, has good views of Great Gable and the Scafells.

THE SUMMIT CAIRN OF RED PIKE, MOSEDALE

Scoat Fell is an undistinguished mass of high land with no pretensions to grace of outline or excitements on its sprawling summit, but it has a key position in the Mosedale Horseshoe, this being the main reason for the ascent. The Ennerdale side of the fell, however, has features of interest, notably the shapely spire of Steeple and the twin coves of Mirk and Mirklin. The view here is of the flat top of the mountain above Mirk Cove with Steeple on the right, taken from the top of Black Crag.

SCOAT FELL

STEEPLE, from Windgap Cove

For years before I ever saw it Steeple's name intrigued me and when finally my wandering brought it within view, the slender spire that my imagination had expected was lacking; the near-vertical tower of rock, however, more than made up for my disappointment. There was obviously no route of ascent on the side facing Windgap Cove although a masochist might well enjoy labouring up the scree gully on the left. The summit, happily, can be reached quite easily from Scoat Fell adjoining.

From the summit ridge of Scoat Fell, Steeple is seen in profile, its east face overlooking Windgap Cove being manifestly impossible, but its neat summit, where one can sit like a king on his throne, can in fact be gained by a mere stroll from the ridge on a clear path. And should be. To be alone on Steeple's tiny top with no other person in sight, is an emotive experience long remembered.

STEEPLE, from Scoat Fell

CRAG FELL

Crag Fell is the western outlier of the range of fells bordering Ennerdale on the south. Approaching from Ennerdale Bridge, a path along the base of the fell accompanies the waterline and is much used; the summit, however, is rarely visited. Anglers Crag is the only obstacle reached on the lakeside path and this was formerly usually circumvented by climbing up and over it although there is no difficulty for active walkers in negotiating the boulders fallen from it and littering the water's edge.

CRAG FELL PINNACLE

At mid-height on the slopes of Crag Fell overlooking Ennerdale Water, there erupts a bizarre group of rock pinnacles around sixty feet in height, vertical fangs apparently resulting from the severe fracturing of a crag in ages past. This is a feature unique in the district and is reached by ascending the fellside immediately above Anglers Crag.

The pools and tarns that bejewel the Lakeland fells have been aptly described as the tears of the mountains. Many occupy secluded hollows, others are familiar landmarks and a few actually appear on the summits, as the one illustrated here. This shallow tarn, a habitat of bog bean and other aquatic plants, is to be found on the top of Grey Knotts above Honister.

THE SUMMIT OF GREY KNOTTS

The tedium of the dusty path to Great Gable from Honister Pass is relieved as it climbs along the side of Grey Knotts by a superlative oversight of the lakes of Buttermere and Crummock Water and the fells sheltering and feeding them. Descending into the valley on the left of this view are Haystacks and High Crag, on the right are the slopes of Fleetwith Pike with Robinson behind, and in the distance bordering Crummock Water is Mellbreak, Low Fell forming the background to a lovely scene.

THE BUTTERMERE VALLEY

There is no fairer scene in Lakeland than the charming valley of
Buttermere, a delight at all times of the year and in any conditions, its
joys undiminished even by rain. The lovely lake, the vivid green pastures
and mature woodlands encompassed by towering heights, contribute to
a picture of romantic beauty unspoilt by the commercialism and crowds
of more accessible parts of the district. May it long remain so.

THE BUTTERMERE VALLEY

A few iron posts still remain of a boundary fence that originally crossed the undulating wasteland between Haystacks and Brandreth, an area confusing in mist and where these scanty survivors give direction. It is known as the Brandreth Fence and as the only landmark has served lost walkers well. In this view Haystacks is in the middle distance beyond the hollow containing Blackbeck Tarn, its cliffs in shadow, and High Crag, a forerunner of the High Stile range, fills the background.

HAYSTACKS AND HIGH CRAG

PILLAR AND HAYSTACKS

On the walk from the top of Honister Pass to Warnscale, passing the abandoned Dubs Quarry, is an arresting view of Green Crag and Haystacks overtopped by Pillar. This walk bypasses the motor road through Honister and, although calling for more effort, is greatly to be preferred.

Haystacks is of daunting appearance, and it must be difficult for anyone who has never climbed to its top to understand the affection so many fellwalkers feel for this savage little monster of a fell. The reason becomes clear only after a personal visit and an exploration of the fascinating labyrinth of features on its broad top, a succession of delightful surprises wherever steps wander. There is a magical lure about Haystacks that brings walkers back time and time again.

HAYSTACKS

INNOMINATE TARN, HAYSTACKS

Haystacks is a mountain small in extent yet abounding in natural features of unique charm that surprise and delight its visitors around every corner. The jewel in the scene is Innominate Tarn, a lonely and lovely sheet of water in a hollow enclosed by heathery undulations and watched over by Great Gable and Pillar.

FLEETWITH PIKE

Buttermere has a glorious surround of fells around the perimeter of the lake, most of them in a continuous line at a high level and not easy to define individually from the lovely shore paths. Only Fleetwith Pike rises in isolation and without doubt of its identity. The climb to its summit along the shadowed facing ridge is rewarded by a superb retrospect of the valley. To the left Honister Pass and its busy traffic runs along the base of the fell, to the right steep slopes descend into Warnscale Bottom; between them is magic.

As height is gained on the climb to Fleetwith Pike the scenic joys of the ascent become more evident with every upward step. Looking back, Buttermere is fully in view, Crummock Water partly, and there is a glimpse of Loweswater in the far distance beyond Mellbreak. Gatesgarth Farm is directly below alongside the Honister Pass road.

BUTTERMERE AND CRUMMOCK WATER

Scarth Gap, at one time more often spelt Scarf Gap, carries a popular path between Buttermere and the head of Ennerdale at Black Sail, so popular in fact that it has needed repair against erosion. The top of the pass is marked by a large cairn and from near this point two other routes diverge, one heading west to High Crag (seen in the picture under mist) for a traverse of the High Stile ridge, the other the short climb to the top of Haystacks.

SCARTH GAP

HIGH CRAG

High Crag is the eastern extremity of the High Stile range, the high ground falling in abrupt scree slopes towards Scarth Gap. This aspect is especially well seen from neighbouring Haystacks, a tiny rock pool just below the summit making an interesting foreground to the scene.

High Stile's towering presence in the Buttermere landscape is seen here from the foothills above the village. The precipitous northeast slope of the mountain, a wild tumble of crags and scree, in shadow for much of the day, falls into the lake, its harshness softened by lakeside plantations. Bleaberry Comb is the upland hollow in sunlight and from it descends the long series of waterfalls in Sour Milk Gill.

HIGH STILE

BURTNESS COMB, HIGH STILE

The High Stile range is deeply scarred on the Buttermere side, the ridge persisting above a succession of mountain hollows known locally as combs. One of these, Bleaberry Comb, is familiar to most walkers as it carries a popular path to Red Pike; another, Burtness (or Birkness) Comb, is ringed by crags and a haunt of rock climbers. In this picture, looking to High Stile from High Crag, Eagle Crag is shadowed and Gray Crag, on the flank of High Stile, is seen in sunlight.

HIGH STILE, from Gatesgarth

The Scots pines on the shore of Buttermere near Gatesgarth make a good foreground to this much-photographed scene overlooked by the lofty peak of High Stile. Although rarely climbed from the head of the lake, a pathless but feasible route can be made from Burtness Comb, the hollow on the left, by following the curving ridge to the summit: a satisfying route for the walker who travels solitary by choice.

One of the joys of fellwalking, a bonus to the healthy exercise and the exhilaration of tramping over rough ground and the satisfaction of reaching lonely summits by one's own efforts, is the wonderful panoramas to be obtained from the high places, aerial views that give perspective to wide landscapes. In this picture Fleetwith Pike is seen rising from the fields of Gatesgarth, its fine west ridge defined by shadow and its highest point still below eye level.

FLEETWITH PIKE, from High Stile

CRUMMOCK WATER, from High Stile

From the cairn on the summit of High Stile there is a glorious aerial view of Crummock Water, seen far below filling the valley between Mellbreak and Grasmoor with Low Fell in the background. High Stile excels in fine views; Pillar is a near neighbour to the south across Ennerdale, and more distantly Great Gable and the Scafells make a classic panorama for the camera.

This arresting view awaits all who visit the summit cairn of High Stile. Bleaberry Tarn in its mountain hollow is seen as birds perceive it, the well-trodden path on its far shore being the popular route to Red Pike. Further, and a thousand feet below the tarn, Crummock Water passes between fellside portals to the Vale of Lorton.

CRUMMOCK WATER AND BLEABERRY TARN

Starling Dodd, here seen from a forest road in Ennerdale, was the final objective in my thirteen-year exploration of the Lakeland fells, and I remember the occasion of my visit very well. It was the last day of the summer bus service to Buttermere and unless I could get to the top that day and make notes of the view, the completion of my work would have to be delayed until the following spring. All went well. I got to the top and there was a clear view but I returned to Buttermere not exuberantly but sadly. It was an end to a very happy experience.

STARLING DODD

FLOUTERN PASS

Most walkers who travel Floutern Pass between Buttemere and Enner-dale will vote this crossing the least attractive of all mountain passes, an extensive tract of very marshy ground being negotiated only at the cost of wet feet. The start and finish of the walk are pleasant, discomfiture occurring in a juicy hollow below Gale Fell. The picture, looking in the direction of Ennerdale, has Great Borne on the left and the miniature Floutern Kop on the right with the path passing between.

Great Borne, also known as Herdhouse or Herdus, is a target for fellwalkers from the coast towns, the ascent usually being made from the top of Floutern Pass, on the left of the photograph. It is prominently in view from Ennerdale Water, where proposals to raise the water level have so far been rightly defeated by conservationists.

GREAT BORNE

MELLBREAK

Mellbreak, although only of modest stature and overtopped by neighbouring heights, displays to the hamlet of Kirkstile nestling in green fields at its base, a formidable and dominating presence, a soaring tower of rock and scree. It looks steep and it is. A stony track, made arduous by loose scree, perseveres to the summit. Halts along the way are justified by the excellence of the views, especially of Loweswater and its environs, and when the top is reached a glorious prospect over the Buttermere valley suddenly unfolds and the toil of the ascent is forgotten.

Mellbreak is particularly well located for views of the valley occupied by Crummock Water and Buttermere and in this one, from a stance below the summit, both lakes are fully displayed to great advantage. The background is formed by the Brandreth ridge beyond Fleetwith Pike leading up to Great Gable. Dale Head is on the far left and the slopes of Red Pike and High Stile fall sharply on the right.

THE BUTTERMERE VALLEY, from Mellbreak

Mellbreak has two tops of similar altitude and a mile apart. Of these the north top is most often visited, being the culmination of the steep ascent from Kirkstile, and presents to those who attain it a delightful aerial vista of Loweswater and, looking over the south top, the peaks around the Buttermere valley in fine array.

THE NORTH SUMMIT OF MELLBREAK

It is a simple walk between the two tops of Mellbreak, pathless but an easy traverse across a grassy depression. The south top is not often visited but from the cairn there is a fine view forward of the slopes of High Stile and Red Pike plunging steeply into the depths of the Buttermere valley and, by a short diversion, beautiful aerial vistas of the lakes of Buttermere and Crummock Water.

THE SOUTH SUMMIT OF MELLBREAK

LOWESWATER

Loweswater, the shyest and least known of the lakes, fits cosily into a
shallow depression in an unspoilt landscape undisturbed by traffic, a
corner of Lakeland that has changed little for two centuries. It is gentle,
not exciting, and happiest when left in solitude. The dominating
mountain hereabouts is Mellbreak and this photograph was taken from
its lower slopes.

THE SUMMIT OF HEN COMB

Hen Comb is a minor fell in stature, without a path to its summit and of little intrinsic interest, yet it commands a splendid view of the mountains enclosing the Buttermere valley, Robinson, Dale Head and Fleetwith Pike being the most prominent heights in the panorama with the lovely lake of Buttermere nestling below. Hen Comb I remember as the only fell I climbed with a companion, a foxhound joining me at the inn at Kirkstile.

Burnbank Fell, on the western fringe of the district above Loweswater, has little of immediate interest but has great merit as a viewpoint for appraising the quiet loveliness of the pastoral countryside around the outflow of Crummock Water and the stark outline of the fells around its shores. In this picture Grasmoor is succeeded by Wandope, Whiteless Pike and Robinson.

BURNBANK FELL

THE LOWESWATER LANDSCAPE, from Lad Hows

From Lad Hows, a shoulder of Grasmoor, there is an uninterrupted view seawards through the gap between the Loweswater fells occupied by the lake and the verdant pastures around Kirkstile. In the far distance is seen the coastal plain and industrial west Cumbria; nearer the viewpoint is the foot of Crummock Water.

The exhilarating ridge walk over Grisedale Pike and Hopegill Head comes to an abrupt end on the top of Whiteside, beyond which the ground falls sharply to Lanthwaite Green. The last part of the ridge from Hopegill Head is here portrayed, a succession of undulations and curves leading to the summit, Whiteside.

WHITESIDE

PASTURES AT KIRKSTILE

Kirkstile is away from the tracks of tourists heading for Buttermere and retains the rural tranquillity that once permeated the whole of Lakeland which has largely been sacrificed by the increasing influx of visitors. These fields between Crummock Water and shy Loweswater are undisturbed by traffic and unspoilt. Life goes on here as it has done for centuries. Kirkstile is Lakeland as it used to be.

Low Fell is accustomed to being bypassed by visitors hurrying to the greater excitement of the Buttermere fells, yet from its modest top is seen a classic view of the full extent of the valley occupied by Crummock Water and Buttermere and the surrounding mountains, the latter being in glorious array overlooking the two lakes. Lanthwaite Hill is the viewpoint of the photograph, the pleasant valley between being threaded by the River Cocker.

LOW FELL, LOWESWATER

HOPEGILL HEAD

Hopegill Head is the finest peak in the northwest of the district, its summit a neat meeting place of interesting ridges above the profound depths of the abyss of Hobcarton Crag, an intimidating precipice defending the habitat of rare botanical specimens and deterring attempts to reach them. This mountain is the central point of an exhilarating traverse from Grisedale Pike to Whiteside and the highlight of the journey.

The fells of the northwest are in general much gentler than those of the
volcanic central region of the district and are smoother underfoot, ideal
territory for the fellwalker, but at Hobcarton Crag the landscape displays
an unusual savagery. A mile-long precipice keeps everyone at bay except
for an occasional intrepid botanist in search of the rare alpine catchfly.

HOBCARTON CRAG

GRASMOOR

No aspect of Grasmoor is more pleasing than that seen across Crummock Water from the eastern slopes of Mellbreak, the cultivated fields of Rannerdale by the lakeside adding brightness to a scene dominated by the untamed mass rising behind. On the right of the picture, with the road to Buttermere running along its base, is the rocky upthrust of Rannerdale Knotts.

Grasmoor's summit is the highest ground in the northwest of Lakeland and consequently commands a far-reaching and extensive panorama, the view across the Buttermere valley and fells to the Scafells and the giants of Ennerdale especially being of a very high order. In other directions the view ranges over a wide area of the district.

THE VIEW FROM GRASMOOR

A pleasant stroll amongst the wooded environs of the outflow of Crummock Water reveals occasional sightings of the mountain dominating the landscape hereabouts and taking the form of a giant pyramid above the farming settlement of Lanthwaite Green.

GRASMOOR, from Lanthwaite Hill

The true proportions of the immense bulk of Grasmoor cannot fully be appreciated from the road along its base, its steep slopes being severely foreshortened and the summit hidden. From Mellbreak, which rises directly opposite across Crummock Water, the details of this southern face of the mountain are clearly revealed and seen to be much too daunting for the average fellwalker to contemplate. The top is attained only by arduous scrambles up the sides or, more easily, from Coledale Hause along the mountain's east ridge.

GRASMOOR

WHITELESS PIKE AND RANNERDALE KNOTTS

The effort of climbing Mellbreak is fully repaid on reaching the summit ridge by a glorious view of the Buttermere valley and, more intimately, of the mountain barrier across Crummock Water directly below. Grasmoor is pre-eminent and to its right rises the more delicately sculptured Whiteless Pike, its facing slope falling very steeply to the rugged foothill of Rannerdale Knotts.

Snow always enhances the stature of the fells, making them truly alpine. Grasmoor's summit is difficult to attain in any conditions from the road along its base; snow-covered, it should be written off as impossible.

GRASMOOR, above Lanthwaite Green

THE SUMMIT OF WANDOPE

Wandope does not rank amongst the best of the northwestern fells and nobody sings its praises, although in Addacombe Hole it has a fine example of a hanging valley. Those who detour to its grassy top, however, enjoy a splendid prospect of the High Stile range overtopped by Pillar. Buttermere fills the valley ahead and identification of the peaks is assisted by the sparkling waters of Bleaberry Tarn.

Skiddaw has a cap of cloud in this winter scene taken from the mine road in Coledale, and patches of snow illuminate the undulating terrrain between. The mine road is a blessing to walkers, enabling the major heights of the northwest to be reached quickly and with little effort from the village of Braithwaite.

COLEDALE

The simple walk along Coledale from Braithwaite is halted at the barytes mine by a precipitous cliff down which pour the twin waterfalls of High Force and Low Force, draining from Coledale Hause. A circuitous path loops to the left to avoid the cliffs and continues to the Hause without hazards but over rather unexciting terrain.

FORCE CRAG, COLEDALE

EEL CRAG AND SAIL

Eel Crag (or Crag Hill as the Ordnance Survey prefers to name it) is most often seen and approached from Coledale where its ramifications are clearly in view. Its opposite face, overlooking the deep cutting of Rigg Beck, is less familiar and less convoluted, appearing as an unbroken parabola of crags above steep slopes. This picture, from Knott Rigg, also shows Sail, a lesser neighbour but with similar characteristics, on the right.

Causey Pike has a peak so pronounced that all fellwalkers in Newlands aspire to reach its summit, there being the invitation and encouragement of a distinct path with only a few rough scrambles near the top. Causey Pike is steeply buttressed by Rowling End, which discloses also the ridge continuing to Eel Crag.

CAUSEY PIKE, from Rowling End

NEWLANDS

There is an enviable peace in the quiet valley of Newlands that makes visitors loth to leave it. The narrow country lanes do not encourage cars, there are no garish signboards to advertise its attractions, there are manifestly no official car parks. It is a backwater par excellence for the fellwalker, having a mountainous surround abounding in delightful high-level expeditions. This view from Rowling End shows High Spy, Dale Head and Hindscarth.

Newlands Hause carries a narrow motor road to Buttermere village from the environs of Keswick, the top of the pass providing parking space for the many cars halting here. The descent there from along the lower slopes of High Snockrigg, a shoulder of Robinson, improves in beauty with every turn of the wheels. Crummock Water appears in the bottom right of the picture, taken from the slopes of Mellbreak.

NEWLANDS HAUSE

Snow always transforms a familiar landscape into a fairyland and when the high fells are out of bounds because of deep drifting, walks along the valleys are a winter delight. Newlands, quieter than ever and free from traffic in such conditions, offers exhilarating walking along its narrow lanes. In this view Catbells and Maiden Moor form the background to a scene of pristine beauty.

NEWLANDS IN WINTER

ROBINSON

Robinson is one of the giants amongst the Buttermere fells but is bulky and lacks grace of outline and fails to impress as do the more delicately sculptured heights opposite across the lake. It is not usually climbed on the side facing the camera although a rough and adventurous way up may be found by a scramble in Goat Gills above Hassness. The easiest route however, starts from Newlands Hause.

Robinson has a descending northeast ridge levelling out on the easy shoulder of High Snab Bank, which in turn drops sharply into the sweet valley of Newlands, the whole offering an obvious route of ascent from the environs of Keswick. A mile-long fringe of cliffs overlooking Newlands Pass accompanies the first part of the descent from the summit.

ROBINSON, from Scope End

NEWLANDS, from Robinson

The descent from Robinson into the sweet valley of Newlands is made doubly enjoyable by the glorious prospect ahead, where Blencathra and Clough Head terminate a wide-ranging and contrasting canvas of natural beauty, the green fields of Newlands shining brightly in a ring of sombre fells.

High Spy above the valley of Newlands is well named. From its rocky top there is a far-reaching view across the district with mountain range succeeding mountain range to end with Helvellyn on the eastern horizon. The solitary walker in the picture is approaching one of the rocky tors that are a feature of this interesting summit.

THE SUMMIT OF HIGH SPY

Dale Head, as seen here from High Spy, presents a fearsome aspect to the upper Newlands valley, which the mountain effectively and abruptly ends, but provides an interesting and adventurous way to the summit, assisted initially by an old cart track to a disused copper mine. In sharp contrast the approach from Honister Pass in the south is a gentle ascent without hazards but lacking excitement until arrival at the summit cairn, when a full-length view of Newlands backed by the distant Skiddaw range explodes upon the eye with stunning effect.

DALE HEAD

THE NORTHWESTERN FELLS, from High Spy

Looking west from High Spy across the great gulf of Newlands the most impressive object in view is the declining ridge of Hindscarth opposite, above uncompromising slopes. Beyond, forming the skyline, are the three peaks of Wandope, Eel Crag and Sail, together offering a fine high-level traverse between the lower part of Newlands and Buttermere.

Dale Head is most easily climbed from Honister Pass but a more exciting and adventurous route lies directly up the north face of the mountain from the head of Newlands valley, where a grassy cart track leads easily upwards to the remains of a copper mine at the foot of Gable Crag. This towering wall of rock can be circumvented on the right to more gentle contours above, the ascent to the summit cairn ending along an airy ridge above the crag.

GABLE CRAG, DALE HEAD

One of the delights of fellwalking on the northwestern fells is the splendid views from their summits and high ridges of the greater heights to the south. Hindscarth is well favoured in this respect having a wide panorama ranging from Bowfell and the Scafell range to Great Gable.

THE SUMMIT OF HINDSCARTH

MAIDEN MOOR

Grange in Borrowdale occupies a lovely situation on the banks of the River Derwent, its charming cottages being the envy of visitors, but the visual appeal of the hamlet and its surroundings is mainly contributed by the sheltering slopes of Maiden Moor which rises immediately beyond in colourful tapestries of grass and heather broken by rocky outcrops and a rim of crags. An enjoyable path traverses the top of the moor.

Derwentwater, from whatever direction it is viewed, always adds beauty to a scene, its lovely wooded bays and headlands having a charm that distinguishes this lake from all others. In this view from the slopes of Maiden Moor, Blencathra is the central height in the background of a scene where land and water are in perfect harmony.

DERWENTWATER, from Maiden Moor

DERWENTWATER, from Maiden Moor

The cairn on the path leading up to the crest of Maiden Moor is accustomed to the clicking of cameras. A full-length view of Derwentwater is on offer with Keswick as an added bonus. Distant Blencathra terminates a view of loveliness in full measure with nothing to mar the harmony of the scene.

The venerable ecclesiastic known as the Bishop, kept in pristine attire by occasional applications of whitewash by his parishioners in the valley below, is an upstanding rock on the steep slopes of Barf above Thornthwaite and can be reached only by a desperate scramble up loose scree, a climb to be recommended only to those who wish to pay reverence to him at close quarters. He is an eye-catching figure to travellers on the newly-aligned A66 alongside and can be seen for miles around. Less respected and now neglected is the Clerk, a smaller rock difficult to identify amongst trees at the base of the fell immediately below.

THE BISHOP OF BARF

CASTLE CRAG, BORROWDALE

Castle Crag is less than a thousand feet in altitude and its ascent is more in the nature of a half-day's ramble than a serious fellwalk. Scramble might be a better word, for its interesting summit is attained only by strenuous effort in the later stages. This modest fell, well endowed with intrinsic charms, is wonderfully situated in the most beautiful part of Lakeland, ringed by higher peaks, and with a sublime view of Derwentwater backed by the Skiddaw group.

The fells in the northwest of Lakeland form a compact and well defined group, different in character but alike in the excellence of the fellwalking they provide, the linking ridges in particular leading to exciting situations. This comprehensive view was taken from the Gale road behind Latrigg.

THE NORTHWESTERN FELLS

Lakeland under snow is a sight denied summer visitors but although the subtler charms of texture and colour are hidden, the landscapes are greatly enhanced by the purity of a white mantle that seems to add height to the mountains and a fresh beauty to the valleys. Winter has always been my favourite season for visiting the district; when the cars and the crowds have departed, silence and peace return and a new magic enchants.

SKIDDAW, from Derwentwater

SKIDDAW, from Bassenthwaite village

Skiddaw's most familiar outline is the one behind Keswick, other aspects of the mountain being less readily recognisable. From the village of Bassenthwaite to the west, the summit appears as a smooth dome buttressed by Broad End, a less exciting challenge but offering routes of ascent, largely pathless, of considerable appeal to adventurous spirits.

Bassenthwaite Lake, the only sheet of water in the district officially named as a lake, is now accompanied by an upgraded A66 on the track of the former railway. The foot of the lake is a yachting centre and from the shores there are uninterrupted views of Skiddaw and its western satellites.

SKIDDAW, from Bassenthwaite Lake

THE SKIDDAW GROUP, from Maiden Moor

The vale of Keswick occupies the middle distance of this view from the slopes of Maiden Moor. The full range of the Skiddaw family is seen beyond from Ullock Pike to Lonscale Fell, Skiddaw and its Little Man being the most prominent. Nearer the camera is Swinside under timber and the sharp peak of Catbells.

Every step of the way from Ullock Pike to the summit of its neighbour Long Side, is a joy to tread. A clear path through patches of heather skirts the edge of a tremendous downfall of screes and rough ground into the little-known valley of Southerndale; southwards is a great array of the mountains around Borrowdale and Newlands. So delightful is this short journey that one reaches the summit cairn on Long Side almost with regret.

LONG SIDE

Much the most interesting route to the summit of Skiddaw lies along the ridge of Ullock Pike and its continuation over the top of Long Side on a path skirting the edge of a precipitous drop into Southerndale and having panoramic views southwards of the mountains encircling Borrowdale. The viewpoint of the picture is Carlside Col from which the final steep ascent to the top of Skiddaw is made over loose screes.

LONG SIDE AND ULLOCK PIKE

THE CARLSIDE COL

The long ravine of Slades Beck almost severs the south side of the Skiddaw massif into two parts. It starts below Carlside Col (the depression between Carl Side and Skiddaw proper) and carves a great gash in the landscape providing a very stony and arid route for walkers but not to be recommended because of its oppressive confines. In the lower stages it meets civilisation under the name of Mill Beck and here is a pleasant watercourse among trees. The picture was taken from the pathless slopes of Skiddaw Little Man.

The summit of Skiddaw Little Man is invariably reached by a short detour from the blazed path to Skiddaw from the Gale road, but may also be ascended directly from the hamlet of Millbeck by a pleasant riverside path upstream. Around a corner where the stream debouches from the stony ravine of Slades Beck, the slope on the right must be tackled without the help of the path and devolves into rather a desperate scramble, although a safe one, with an exhilarating finish.

SKIDDAW LITTLE MAN

The northern fells have never had the popular appeal of the rest of Lakeland but their remoteness and undisturbed tranquillity are inducements to walkers who prefer lonely summits and wilderness landscapes. This picture shows the spectacular waterfall of Whitewater Dash, its secluded setting amongst unfrequented fells with the rough road to Skiddaw House contouring above it on the right.

DASH FALLS

The saddle linking the summit of Blencathra with Foule Crag and which gives the mountain the alternative name of Saddleback, is here seen overtopping Scales Fell; from Foule Crag there is a glimpse of Sharp Edge descending on the right. Opposite the viewpoint are the bland grassy slopes of Bannerdale Crags with the valley of the River Glenderamackin curving around the base.

BLENCATHRA, from Mousthwaite Col